BREAKING
FREE

Living free of the

Opinions of others

BREAKING FREE

Living free of the

Opinions of others

By Jacqueline Rhymes

Destiny House Publishing, LLC

Detroit, MI

Breaking Free

Living Free of the Opinions of Others

Published by Destiny House Publishing, LLC

Copyright ©2013 Jacqueline Rhymes

ISBN-

978-1936867707

Unless otherwise stated, all scripture quotations are from the Holy Bible, King James Version. Scripture references that do not have the Bible version noted are the author's paraphrase.

Editing: Cover design and Publication

Layout: Destiny House Publishing, LLC

Artwork:

Printed in the United States of America

For information:

Destiny House Publishing, LLC

www.destinyhousepublishing.com

Email: inquiry@destinyhousepublishing.com

P.O. Box 19774

Detroit, MI 48219 -888-890-9455

FORWARD

This is a must read for those who desire and seek change and increase in their lives.

Prophetess Rhymes takes you on a journey that will bring you to a place of healing and wholeness; free you from the dependency of needing acceptance from others.

This book provides spiritual and personal insights on the complexity of living by the opinion of others. The author is transparent about her personal journey to be free from the opinion of others. It will make you think, cry and understand how you arrived at a place of dependency; but most of all teach you how to recover and be made free.

MINISTER MARY WILBON

ORDAINED OF GOD FULL GOSPEL MINISTRIES

CHICAGO, ILLINOIS

CONTENTS

INTRODUCTION

BREAKING FREE

FROM THE COLLISIONS OF LIFE

Breaking free is the ability to shatter the glass ceilings that have been placed over your life, namely by the person in the mirror, you. I would like to compare it to a collision. When something collides it usually causes damages, some worse than others, and as a result of the collision, usually something gets shifted from its original condition. This book is about breaking free from self-inflicted collisions in your life. It will help you understand what has been interrupting you from becoming who you were created to become.

I believe that if you are reading this book, it is because you have had some collisions and impacts in your life. You have probably had some rear-enders, some things that hit you from behind. Rear-enders are those things that catch you off guard or leave you in a position of vulnerability. Then there are the fender-benders where you were at fault. These are usually the hardest to accept because being at fault is something with which we often struggle with. The truth of the matter is that there is no one to blame but you. It is always easier to place blame than to be the blame. And lastly, you have even had a few pile ups, where more than one thing hit you at once. Pile ups are those things that hit you in multiple areas; your health, your marriage, your children, your self-esteem, and your finances. I could continue on but only you know the multiple hits you have taken. These collisions can leave you damaged and fragmented. Unfortunately, many of the things that have happened are the results of those things that you have given permission too.

This book helps you take a serious look at the collisions in your life and allow you to get a glimpse of what you have permitted to enter in and taken precedence over your God given assignments.

CHAPTER 1

WHO ARE YOU?

Often people tell me that their problem is not a lack of confidence. Yet, when asked about themselves who they are, I am given titles rather than characteristics. **(Characteristic – a feature or quality that makes somebody or something recognizable – Encarta Dictionary)**

What makes you recognizable? What makes people identify you from others? Truly there are many mothers, fathers, husbands, wives, etc., but what is the uniqueness that separates you? What makes you an original? If your titles were stripped away, who would be left standing? I challenge you; do you even know who you are outside of your titles? If you cannot give yourself three answers quickly about who you are without having to research and ponder than I am sad to report, you probably don't know yourself. (Selah).

It's time for a moment of truth. Ask yourself these questions, how important is it that people like me? Accept who I am? Approve of what I do? How often do you ask others what they think about your ideas? Freedom only comes when you can be honest with yourself. The first step to freedom is becoming transparent with you.

Everything stems from you knowing who you are. Find your identity and you will find your destiny.

Allow yourself to celebrate your sense of freedom your capacity to make a choice and your strength in facing the truth. Not everyone has the courage to do so even if it hurts... **knowing** is the key to acceptance – **ABBY ESPIRETRE**

Jesus asked the question who do men say I am
Matt 16:13-18MSG

13 When Jesus arrived in the villages of Caesarea Philippi, he asked his disciples, "What are people saying about who the Son of Man is?" **14** They replied, "Some think he is John the Baptizer, some say Elijah, some Jeremiah or one of the other prophets." **15** He pressed them, "And how about you? Who do you say I am?" **16** Simon Peter said, "You're the Christ, the Messiah, the Son of the living God." **17** Jesus came back, "God bless you, Simon, son of Jonah! You didn't get that answer out of books or from teachers. My Father in heaven, God himself, let you in on this secret of who I really am. **18** And now I'm going to tell you who you are, really are. You are Peter, a rock. This is the rock on which I will put together my church, a church so expansive with energy that not even the gates of hell will be able to keep it out.

When Peter got a revelation of whom Jesus was he was able to get knowledge of who he was. The multitude will always think you are

11

something other than who God has called you to become. When Peter, by the Spirit, identified who Jesus was - he was told who he was. It is only through our persistent pursuit of God that we understand who we really are and what we have been called to become.

Esther was just an orphan girl in the embryonic stage of her destiny. She didn't know that her life was going to take a drastic turn and that her destiny was meant to become queen. In the eyes of men, Esther was just an orphan that Mordecai was raising. If you would have asked them, they would have said, "That is Esther, the orphan relative of Mordecai." Except God reveals, it is impossible for man to know the destiny God has planned for your life.

I can imagine what she had to endure, days of feeling like an outsider, even though she was loved by her uncle. There were some days that she probably felt like where she was represented the sum of her life; never imagining that God had a plan for her that was bigger than her greatest imagination.

> **Jeremiah 29:11TLB**
>
> **11** For I know the plans I have for you," says the Lord. "They are plans for good and not for evil, to give you a future and a hope.

Thomas Edison was the youngest of 7 siblings. He had poor health in his early years, and developed scarlet fever. Some believe this led to his poor hearing and eventually to total deafness. He was considered a poor student and it is said he heard his teacher call him addle or slow. His mother (a teacher) took him out of school and home schooled him. He was an ardent reader with a great curiosity; he had a fascination for mechanical things and chemicals.

Yet in the eyes of some of those that were responsible for impacting his life, he was looked at as being slow, without the potential to accomplish anything great in his life. He was considered sub-standard. Thank God for a mother who saw the great wealth in him.

Regardless of what you have had to overcome, God will always send someone into your life to speak of the great wealth of potential that's in you. In Edison's lifetime, he had 1,093 patents. It is evident that his teacher didn't see the potential in him.

DISCOVERING YOU

How important is it that people like you, accept who you are and approve of what you do?

How often do you ask others about your ideas, or visions?

What makes you recognizable? What makes people identify you from others?

If all your titles were taken away, who would you be?

Inspired Thoughts...

_____

_____

_____

_____

_____

_____

_____

_____

_____

_____

_____

_____

_____

_____

_____

_____

_____

_____

_____

Inspired Thoughts...

_____
_____
_____
_____
_____
_____
_____
_____
_____
_____
_____
_____
_____
_____
_____
_____
_____
_____
_____
_____

THE IMPACT OF FINDING ACCEPTANCE

Discovering your co-dependencies and addictions can be a hard thing to face. You might be shocked that I used the word addiction, but that's what seeking approval is. Addiction is defined as the state of being enslaved to a habit or practice, a strong craving. An extreme need for attention and acceptance operates like an addiction. It forms a habit, a practice or craving for approval on every level of life; in your home, on your job, in your relationships. Like a drug the more you indulge in this behavior, the more you have to have this approval. It is imperative that you understand that this dependency is like a pressure cooker. It breaks down your mental, physical, social and spiritual makeup.

The impact of trying to find acceptance can paralyze and put your life on hold and even end your destiny. Many have had their life suspended and rendered ineffective because they were seeking approval. This impact can be devastating if there is an unwillingness to learn from past experiences. These experiences are morsels left to guide you to reality, and cause you to look at your condition. You must ask yourself these questions, what is the affect that others have on me? Do you concern yourself how they look at you? How far are you willing to go to find acceptance?

1 Sam 15:24ASB

24 Then Saul said to Samuel, "I have sinned; I have indeed transgressed the command of the Lord and your words, because I feared the people and listened to their voice.

Although King Saul was among the people, he had been elevated to lead them. But his need to stay among them, limited him in his assignment. His mission was altered because of his need to be accepted by the people he was called to lead.

The spirit of rejection is a tool often used by the enemy, coupled by its cousin fear. The combination of the two can be explosive in your life causing you to alter your destiny.

> Courage is not the absence of fear but rather the judgment that something else is more important than fear. **JAMES NEIL HOLLINGWORTH**

Take inventory of what is more important than your greatest fears. It is only when you are able to identify what is more important and take courage, that you will be able to move forward, Know that fear itself cannot stop you; it is when you refuse to move in the midst of it, that brings defeat.

DISCOVERING YOU

What is the impact others have on you?

What is the depth of your dependence on others opinion?

Make a list of what is more important than your greatest fears?

Inspired Thoughts...

_____

_____

_____

_____

_____

_____

_____

_____

_____

_____

_____

_____

_____

_____

_____

_____

_____

_____

_____

_____

_____

_____

THE CORD THAT NO LONGER NOURISHES

The most difficult separation is to move from where you have been to where you are going. A lack of self-confidence in your purpose will cause you to cling to those that have been a part of your beginning, even when you know that this is no longer a productive season in your life.

Please don't misunderstand me, I'm not dealing with not loving, respecting or caring about a person, but when you talk about destiny and the next level everyone cannot get you there. There are those that have been placed in your life to get you to a certain place. But that is as far as their influence and knowledge can take you.

God showed me in a dream many years ago a baby that looked like it was one year old. It was still attached to the umbilical cord and the baby was gray. Immediately I knew that God was saying that what was once a growth process was now a lifeless one and the cord of dependence had to be severed in order to continue to thrive and live. This is the hardest separation because of all you have learned and gained from this mentor.

When God pushes you out of the nest it is to teach you to fly alone for a season. I believe that there are many mentors that God will send your way; but you have to be willing to detach from the old so that you will be able to receive the new. The old often has a different outlook on the new thing that God is doing in your life.

In this season, God is teaching you to hear his voice and obey above the multitude of those from your past.

DISCOVERING YOU

Where are you going?

What do you need to get there?

Do you recognize your mentors? How willing are you to submit to them?

Inspired Thoughts...

_____
_____
_____
_____
_____
_____
_____
_____
_____
_____
_____
_____
_____
_____
_____
_____
_____
_____
_____
_____
_____
_____

CHAPTER 2

PEOPLE PLEASERS

"If God were our one and only desire, we would not be so easily upset when our opinions do not find outside acceptance." – **THOMAS KEMPIS**

The problem with Saul and many others is the danger of being popular with people. Many are stifled in life because of the great fear of being rejected by people. Fear is one of the most controlling spirits that one can be bound by, it is said that fear is false evidence appearing real. It leaves you with a false visual of what could happen if you don't succumb to its false realities. It stifles dreams and destinies. Everything that God had for Saul was relinquished because of his fear of man.

PROVERBS 29:25 MSG – The fear of human opinion disables; trusting in GOD, protects you from that.

 Overly saturating yourself with what others think about you can restrict, stop, and disqualify you from what God has chosen you to do. Throughout the ages man has been hindered by the desperate need for man's acceptance.

Saul's need to be accepted by people outweighed his obedience to God. This type of person is known as a people pleaser. People pleasers are those that constantly go against what they believe and know is right to get along with others.

People often get upset when you tell them they are people pleasers. Yet when they begin to give a description of what their life is like, it is full of compromises. Being a people pleaser is not just saying yes, but the willingness to compromise one's belief by trying to please others.

There are levels of compromise. (1) Accepting less (2) Going against one's belief (3) Accepting what is not wanted. What is the level of your compromise?

People Pleasers often feel that compromise will cause them to be loved and accepted by others. So they are willing to put up with things that they would have otherwise rejected. They are willing to go against what they do not morally support. There are those that are willing to compromise their own beliefs to get along with others. I have seen people that don't drink, allow drinking to go on at their various functions. Why? Because they want to please people by keeping the peace (even though the choice went against their own beliefs). There are people that sacrifice time, energy, and money to have others accept them. They are afraid to say no to most requests that are placed before them. They are willing to do things they don't want to do all for one purpose - acceptance. Have you found yourself in dread, yet in agreement? You are dreading what you are doing yet you are in agreement for approval.

Are you doing things with a smile, but in your heart you have no desire or pleasure in your undertakings? It's all because of your need to be accepted.

DISCOVERING YOU

What are you in dread of, yet in agreement with?

LEVELS OF COMPROMISE:

How often do you accept less and why?

Are you willing to go beyond your convictions to find agreement?

How often do you accept what is not wanted?

Inspired Thoughts...

_____

_____

_____

_____

_____

_____

_____

_____

_____

_____

_____

_____

_____

_____

_____

_____

_____

_____

_____

_____

_____

_____

Inspired Thoughts...

_____

_____

_____

_____

_____

_____

_____

_____

_____

_____

_____

_____

_____

_____

_____

_____

_____

_____

_____

HOLDING A FALSE BURDEN

Duty, obligation, weight, responsibility, and worry are all a part of carrying a burden. We often carry things for which we are not responsible. King Saul was not responsible for the opinions of the people; He was responsible for obedience to his assignment. He picked up pressure and a burden that had not been sanctioned by God, but man. I want to deal with your insecurities, your lack of confidence to do your assignment. People withdraw from their assignment because they don't feel they can go through the pressure of what it takes to complete their mission. If you find yourself not being able to say no or resist moving forward due to things that resist you and your purpose than you are sabotaging your own future.

You cannot be afraid to lose, you cannot be afraid to be friendless. You cannot be afraid of not having enough. You cannot allow fear to grip you. When the weightiness of people outweighs your responsibility to God, you will always set yourself in motion to abort the will of God.

Are the burdens of people's opinions over-riding your obedience to God's will for your life? When you are intimidated by man's opinion of you, it is easy to fall into disobedience with God. The scripture reminds us that "Fearing people is a dangerous trap...**Proverb 29:25NTL**" Saul feared how he would look in the sight of the people more than how his actions would be disapproved in the sight of God. Time and time again, we see where people failed because they made decisions based on the opinion of others and not on their convictions.

DISCOVERING YOU

What things are you carrying that you are not responsible for?

What are you allowing to pressure you?

After careful evaluation, are you carrying a false burden, if so how are you going to handle relieving yourself of this burden?

Inspired Thoughts...

_____
_____
_____
_____
_____
_____
_____
_____
_____
_____
_____
_____
_____
_____
_____
_____
_____
_____
_____
_____
_____

Inspired Thoughts...

_____
_____
_____
_____
_____
_____
_____
_____
_____
_____
_____
_____
_____
_____
_____
_____
_____
_____
_____
_____
_____

CHAPTER 3

SETTLING FOR LESS

You have heard the phrase "the elephant in the room", implying that there is something in the room that's occupying the majority of the space, and everyone is ignoring this big animal as though he was not there.   Settling for acceptance is like the elephant in the room, you find yourselves allowing your need for acceptance to occupy the majority of your space so that what you really desire cannot come in.

Trying to find acceptance often leads to settling for something other than what you want.   Have you ever settled for something different because you were told something else was better for you? It could have been the simplest thing as shopping for clothing; you try on something and its okay , not quite what you really had in mind, but because someone said that looks good on you , you accepted it and later got home and left it in your closet because that is not really what you wanted.

It takes boldness and courage to over-ride the opinions of men and stand in your own skin. It is time to take a hard look at you. And be true to thine own self. What things am I accepting that I really don't want? Could it be that God has called you to something that others cannot see or accept, but the fear of not being accepted has stifled your growth progress and success?

Settling for less is often a result of not having the faith to believe waiting for God is better. Therefore, many have accepted the lesser thing, when the greater was available.

> Once you say you're going to settle for less that's what happens to you in life
>
> **(John F. Kennedy)**

Settling for less causes you to live a life in second place, you might say second place is not so bad but second place is not your best life. Settling for less leaves you living a passionless life. You accept positions or, careers not based on your potential but on the number of zeroes on your pay check. You accept careers that have been determined by others but lacking the passion to give all of yourself in it. You accept marriages that have no love, perhaps because you felt time was running out and you were afraid to be alone, or maybe you did it because you were looking for financial security, and the lowest state is that you did it for sex. Then there are those that are in ministry that are Pastors that should have been Evangelists, and Prophets that should have been Teachers but in the eyes of men these positions where of greater value, but for you it was accepting the lessor. What good is it to be a mediocre Pastor when you could be a powerful anointed Evangelist? What good is it to have a career that others are deprived of your excellence, or to be married and yet not happy.

All of these things are received, not out of purpose   but out of acceptance, because someone said this is what you are supposed to have or supposed to be doing.   If you do not have a perspective on what God wants and what you want, your life will be full of acceptance rather than God inspired desires. You will embrace and accept what does not bring you full freedom and joy, for the purpose of being accepted.   Stop and ask yourself why I am living in someone else's dreams and not my own. Am I so desperate for attention that I would take on the life of someone other than my own, and live out their passions and not my own?

> Never settle for less than you deserve, because that's when you lose not only your happiness, but lose yourself **(Unknown quote)**

DISCOVERING YOU

What is the elephant in your room?

How often do you settle for what you don't want?

Take inventory of your wants and what you don't want

Inspired Thoughts...

_____
_____
_____
_____
_____
_____
_____
_____
_____
_____
_____
_____
_____
_____
_____
_____
_____
_____
_____
_____
_____
_____
_____

IS IT ALRIGHT NOW?

This is the question often asked in the mind of those that struggle with being accepted. Is what I am doing all right to you, now??? Is everything I have become, acceptable to you, now? Do you find yourself mounting your life up on the approval of others? Are you often asking is it alright now? There are people in relationships that have changed their entire personality to find acceptance in others.

Many long for approval and acceptance. They have a need to know, 'Am I doing it right?'

It is not wrong to desire healthy acceptance. A child desires the approval of a parent, a husband to a wife, and a wife to a husband. It is the place of neediness that is the danger. Those that sacrifice themselves constantly and give into the demands of others often find themselves battling with bitterness and anger because they realize that all they have done neither satisfies or appeases the other person(s).

In all of the acceptance that has been rendered toward man have you stopped to ask the more important question, "God, is it all right with you? Lord, are you pleased with my life?" These questions will eliminate the fear of not being all right with people.

In **Genesis 29:31-35** – You find the story of Leah, the wife that was not accepted by her husband Jacob because she was not his choice.   Jacob was in love with her sister Rachel.   Leah did everything to get the approval of her husband.   She thought she would find acceptance with her husband by giving him sons.   Each son she thought surely it will be alright with him now, because after all she was giving him something that her sister could not produce.

Genesis 29:33-35-MSG

33 She became pregnant again and had another son. "God heard," she said, "that I was unloved and so he gave me this son also." She named this one Simeon (God-Heard). **34** She became pregnant yet again — another son. She said, "Now maybe my husband will connect with me — I've given him three sons!" That's why she named him Levi (Connect). **35** She became pregnant a final time and had a fourth son. She said, "This time I'll praise God." So she named him Judah (Praise-God). Then she stopped having children.

You have to make a decision in life that it's not about what is alright with people, but God is it alright with you. Leah spent a large portion of her life with disappointments and feeling like a failure, because she felt she could not get approval from her husband. Her whole life was based on producing to make him happy and fulfilled until finally she realize it was time to give God Praise, it no longer mattered what Jacob thought. She came to herself that there was greatness in her whether he ever approved of her. She saw the evidence produced out of her. What about you regardless of what man will acknowledge about you, can you see the greatness that is being produced out of your life. Take another look it's there!

DISCOVERING YOU

What is it about you that lack the confidence to believe in you?

What have you sacrificed to make it alright with others?

How often have you asked God is it alright with him?

Are you happy with you?

Inspired Thoughts...

_____

_____

_____

_____

_____

_____

_____

_____

_____

_____

_____

_____

_____

_____

_____

_____

_____

_____

_____

_____

_____

Inspired Thoughts...

_____

_____

_____

_____

_____

_____

_____

_____

_____

_____

_____

_____

_____

_____

_____

_____

_____

_____

_____

_____

_____

OUCH THAT HURTS –

THE SHOE THAT DOESN'T FIT

> I didn't try to copy my dad or fit into the mold that everybody tried to make me fit into – **JOEL OSTEEN**

We are sometimes afraid to be different because we want to fit in. It's like wearing a shoe that is too small because we like how it looks. We are willing to undergo the pain, so we adjust our comfort for discomfort, walking around with a look good but not a feel good. We adapt to a mirage appearing to be a size 8 when we are a size 9. Life can be like the shoes I just described. You can become addicted to adjusting and adapting your life to something that doesn't fit. We love how acceptance looks but not always how it makes us feel. We often repress, the development of our own gifting's, and try to squeeze into someone else's gifting because we want to be accepted. Our private desire is that people are able to see our gifting's, our potential and motivate us to continue on. We look for a positive response to join in and fit in.

Being accepted by others can give you a sense of acceptance on the outside, but often leave you empty on the inside. You will find yourself battling from the awkwardness of trying to squeeze into a place that doesn't fit. Have you ever been in a place and you felt like you were on the outside looking in? You found yourself fighting to find a comfortable place to fit. In that place you are usually operating from the outside, which brings a discomfort on the inside, because it is not you, it's not who you were designed to be. In those instances, you are reluctant to say too much, because you don't know if it will be accepted. You are afraid to be different, sound different, and look different; so like on an assembly line you march to the beat of what has been adjusted by man's standards, and not God's.

This book is not embracing any sinful lifestyles you have adapted. But the person that God speaks of in you.

Jeremiah 1:4-5-AMP **4** Then the word of the Lord came to me [Jeremiah], saying, **5** Before I formed you in the womb I knew [and] approved of you [as My chosen instrument], and before you were born I separated and set you apart, consecrating you; [and] I appointed you as a prophet to the nations.

In other words, God has purpose for your life. I ask you this question, who has been writing on your life's pages that has deferred the purpose of God in your life? When you entered this world each of us came in empty. Many people have made deposits in your life, which have played a part in shaping your identity, some were shaping's that had been orchestrated by God and others were meant to keep you from purpose.

Jeremiah 29:11-NIV For I know the plans I have for you declares the Lord; plans to prosper you and not harm you, plans to give you a hope and future.

Has your personality and your self-worth been entangled with wrong perspectives about yourself based on a lack of positive mentoring.

It is God's desire that you allow Him to untangle the negative input that has been instilled in you. Like Jeremiah, he has a plan for your life. Allow yourself to become free from the stronghold of the opinions of men.

DISCOVERING YOU

How much of your life are you adjusting to things that don't fit?

Are you depending on others to define your gifting's?

Are you with the wrong group?

Inspired Thoughts...

_____
_____
_____
_____
_____
_____
_____
_____
_____
_____
_____
_____
_____
_____
_____
_____
_____
_____
_____
_____
_____
_____
_____
_____

CHAPTER 4

BREAKING THE GLASS

> Break the glass – I thought to myself because it is a symbolic gesture. Try to understand that within myself, things were breaking of much more importance than a glass and I'm happy for that. Look to your own inner struggles and break this glass. – **AUTHOR UNKNOWN**

Breaking the glass is an expression used when something that has held you has been broken. Breaking the glass is shattering false perceptions and mindset of who you are, and who you are to become. Shattering unhealthy mindsets is essential in order for you to come out of the confining glass that has posed limitations and stagnation in your growth and maturity.

Many have been delivered out of their confinement, but are still not free. You must understand that you can be delivered but not free. You can be delivered from your captivity and hardship, yet in your mind there is no freedom, because you are living in the shadows of others, and even though you are no longer bound you are not free in your assessment of yourself; because it is based on the opinions of people.

The Bible says whom the Son makes free is free indeed. Jesus has broken the glass that confines you. Now you have to find out who you are and walk in the freedom that has been granted to you. Every day you will be challenged with something or someone that will oppose your new freedom. You must arrest every old thought by the word of God in order to maintain your liberty.

<u>DISCOVERING YOU</u>

Make a list of the inner struggles that need to be broken inside of you.

Coming out of your confined place means you doing what?

Find scriptures to support your freedom.

Inspired Thoughts...

_____

_____

_____

_____

_____

_____

_____

_____

_____

_____

_____

_____

_____

_____

_____

_____

_____

_____

_____

_____

_____

_____

TAKING A RISK

Risk comes from not knowing what you are doing – **WARREN BUFFET**

When you find your path you must ignore fear.   You need to have the courage to risk mistakes, but once you are on that road…run, run, run, and don't stop till you've reached its end – **JOSE N. HARRIS**

You must be willing to take a risk on your own plans and ideas that you believe God inspired you to do.   I challenge you to dare to trust what you hear and what you see and have a resolve to stand firm in it.   Even in writing this book there is a temptation to stop and get approval, but I know that I have to finish this assignment before anyone can truly be helped. This book is my risk.

If you are going to release the potential within you, you must be willing to take a risk. You have to do something without knowing the outcome. There is a possibility, your ideas and your plans might not be accepted. But there is a greater possibility that you will begin to look at your life as full instead of empty. You will never achieve your highest goals being pessimistic. Change the way you think and you will be able to take the risk. See the glass half full instead of half empty. Dare to go beyond what you see in front of you. Greatness is fueled by risks. Life is full of risks that pull you out of your safety net.

Releasing your safety net to become what you were created to be is one of the most powerful achievements you can ever obtain. Myles Munroe said (paraphrasing) "The graveyard is a place full of the most unfulfilled potentials". There is a level of comfort that has to be released in order to become you. That means all of the things that you have held on to as your safety net: your shyness that you say is just you, your abrasive behavior, your inability to communicate are all smoke screens to keep you from reaching your destiny. Speak life to yourself and release all your insecurities to become you. The life of the caterpillar is a great example of releasing to become.

DISCOVERING YOU

What are you willing to risk for your ideas and plans?

What does taking a risk mean to you?

What are your safety nets?

Inspired Thoughts...

_____

_____

_____

_____

_____

_____

_____

_____

_____

_____

_____

_____

_____

_____

_____

_____

_____

_____

_____

_____

_____

TRANSFORMATION

You've got to be a caterpillar before you are a butterfly, the problem is, most people are not willing to be a caterpillar - **UNKNOWN**

The caterpillar has within it, everything it needs to become a beautiful butterfly, but to become different it must make a sacrifice for what it will become. You must outlast your present to see your future. Some caterpillars die in their caterpillar state while others progress into a new life and change from their present existence. The process of this transformation is not easy. The caterpillar must allow itself to be stripped of what it is use to, and deny its present state. How willing are you to be stripped from your present state?

The process sometimes deters many from the change. The caterpillar must go through what seems like an idle time of doing nothing while it is being formed anew.

Like the caterpillar I am in a waiting tank, I am waiting for some things to change, but I realize that change has to happen on the inside first. My insides are waiting to give birth to my true self. I find myself sitting on a limb.

My difficulty started with trying to cover a problem. I got a sew-in to cover the thinning of my hair and ended up in a worst state. I then went from a sew-in to glue, which has left me in a graver state, completely bald in the top. There is nothing wrong with weave, this process does not affect everyone in this manner. I believe there is purpose behind everything that happens in life. What has taken place with me has revealed a deeper problem then losing hair, it was my deep concern of how others would see me.

Your situation may not be mine but have you ever created a bigger problem because you used the wrong method to solve the first problem.

My thoughts were to come away from what I was use to and accept the fact that the only way I might achieve my change was to come out of the weave, so that my hair would be able to breathe, get healthy and possibly grow again. My decision has taken time, and patience. Time is something that we can embrace or dread.

Most Christians are unsuccessful in their change, because of the process of time. Time can be a killer or a motivator depending on how you look at life. If you believe your state of doing nothing is just a time of preparation you will have peace in your change. But if you look at time itself it can become a hindrance to change. You must count your time of sitting as an opportunity to become or do something that you have never experienced.

When I first started my process, I was plagued with many concerns. Will my hair come back strong, and healthy? Will I be able to wear color? Will the wigs look attractive, on me? I pondered all of these questions, but the choice was mine. No one could help me in the decision. I had to be willing to take the risk without any certain returns.

I will share with you, what the Holy Spirit spoke to me. As my stylist and I were discussing the process of change, the Holy Spirit began to minister to me that if I wanted change I had to become like the caterpillar. My first response was not to share what I had just heard with my stylist, because I was not sure that I could do it. I wrestled with a lot of different thoughts that included what if I tell her and then I don't do it? What would she think about me as a woman of God or a woman of faith? You see sometimes silence can keep you from moving forward. I shared what was uncomfortable to the caretaker of my hair and she encouraged me to do what I already knew I had to do. Once I made up my mind, the next step was to share with my husband what I had decided to do. I had told him about my baldness, but he had never seen it before. I was concerned that I would no longer look attractive to him. How would I feel walking around the house revealed? He assured me that he loved me. He even volunteered to go bald also.

I challenge you, what decisions do you need to make, that you are afraid of allowing the real you to be seen? Changing involves risks. You have to be willing to be in a place of discomfort for a season. Like me, you can make all kinds of excuses. But when it all boiled down, I realized I was fearful that what I was about to do was going to make me less attractive, in the eyes of others. The Bible says as a man thinketh in his heart so is he.

How true the word is! I thought in my own eyes I was unattractive with no hair. I know my husband loves me very much but the thought of him seeing me bald was more than concerning. I had described my hair loss to him but had never allowed him to see my baldness. When I first lost my hair, I was even embarrassed for other women in the salon to see my baldness. The Holy Spirit challenged me; you see my problem was not with my hair but with how I looked at myself. In a still soft voice, the Holy Spirit challenged me with this simple matter. "Can you hang on a limb and risk not looking the way you want to look?

The next phase was going to church in my new look. The color was different and the style. I found myself wishing I would have started this process on a day that I didn't have to minister. Again, I was concerned about what people would think, and even what some might say. The thoughts the enemy had suggested in my mind never happened. It was up to me to perceive truth about my situation. I realized that what I was feeling were only inner distractions. If I could not conquer my inner thoughts I would never be able to be free from my outer emotional challenges.

Ask yourself, "How bad do you want to become all that you have been created to become? Or is the fear of the process enough to keep you bound in an old life. If you are saying things like it's too hard, it's too much you are conditioning yourself to stay the same. You have to be willing to be uncomfortable and perhaps inconvenienced for a season to receive change. Change is not handed on a silver platter.

The last stage of the process for the caterpillar is to break out of the cocoon. Breaking out of what you have been wrapped in, takes strength, and courage, the comfort of being idle, but protected can become a handicap. Although the new has arrived it will not come forth without one last effort to find its way out.

Like the caterpillar soon to become the butterfly, although you may be close, you have to have the strength and endurance to give yourself one last push in what you have been wrapped in, in order to function in your full potential.

I am giving myself the last push because I realized in order to break free I had to do something. I have sought medical help to assist me in my transition. This process has proven to be lengthy, costly, and without any natural returns. I have accepted and embraced my change. What I wanted to receive did not manifest in the natural, but what God wanted me to receive has been a great wealth of spiritual return. It has opened me up in ways that I never imagined. You see when the Holy Spirit spoke to me and asked the question could I hang on a limb for a season, I thought He (The Holy Spirit) was talking about hair. The Bible says in Isaiah 55:8 my thoughts are not your thoughts neither are my ways your ways. Hair was only the means used to get me to my place of healing and deliverance. It unlocked all the hidden places of insecurities within me and gave me an understanding of me. I am thankful that a physical condition has brought me to an inner healing.

DISCOVERING YOU

How are you looking at time?

What do you need to do to take the last push?

How bad do you want to become you? What steps do you need to take?

Inspired Thoughts...

_____

_____

_____

_____

_____

_____

_____

_____

_____

_____

_____

_____

_____

_____

_____

_____

_____

_____

_____

_____

_____

CHAPTER 5

FINDING YOUR PATH

Finding your way can be a challenge because for a long time you have been on paths that were not leading you to your destiny. They were paths that were sustainable; but not capable of leading you to your destined path.

The danger of these paths is that you can settle there because they are workable, they support you, they are viable.

When we look at the story of Joseph we find that he was on many paths and even though they looked like unprofitable paths, God always gave him favor in the midst of seemingly bad situations. It would have been easy for him to settle at Potiphar's house where he was living quite comfortably, but God allowed situations to arise at each path to allow him to get back on his destined path. Although he was favored at each path, he could not stay at those paths and walk into his destiny

You must understand that although you can accomplish many tasks, there is only one that is your ultimate purpose. You can be good at something but not great. I can sing but I'm not an accomplished psalmist. All other paths are just in-roads to that path. They are only paths that are intended to prepare you for your outcome.

If you are not careful, you can stop at an in-road and think this is what you are supposed to be doing, this is as far as you can go. If you believe this, you will spend the rest of your life living in the shadow of something that does not lead to your ultimate purpose.

Finding your path is one of determination. You cannot take the easy route to get there. You cannot settle for seconds when God has called you to be first. You must be willing to blaze trails that have not yet been traveled. Your uniqueness will lead you along the least traveled path but if you have the courage to be you, the path will bring you the confidence that you have so longed for, the courage that you have prayed for, the creativity that has been trapped in you by the opinions of men.

DISCOVERING YOU

What paths are you on?

Are your paths in-roads?

Do you know when you get there?

Inspired Thoughts...

_____
_____
_____
_____
_____
_____
_____
_____
_____
_____
_____
_____
_____
_____
_____
_____
_____
_____
_____
_____
_____
_____
_____

THE PLACE OF DELIVERY

> The power and intensity of your contractions cannot be stronger than you, it is you — **UNKNOWN**

Your pain is coming from you and you are stronger than your pain so push your way out. The way you look at your delivery will change how you give birth to it.

It's your appointed time to push out of the cocoon. The scripture says:

Isaiah 66:9-TLB

9 Shall I bring to the point of birth and then not deliver?" asks the Lord your God. "No! Never!

Not only is it necessary to come forth at the appointed time, but it takes strength and endurance to break forth. You must use your own strength to become the new you. You have waited. You have cried. You have prepared. Now, push. The reward out-weighs the difficulty. When it is time to give birth, don't be fearful of coming out, don't be afraid of being a different frame than what others have framed you.

DISCOVERING YOU

What are you getting ready to give birth to?

Are you preparing for delivery?

Your delivery time depends on your cooperation how are you cooperating with your process?

Inspired Thoughts...

_____
_____
_____
_____
_____
_____
_____
_____
_____
_____
_____
_____
_____
_____
_____
_____
_____
_____
_____
_____
_____

FREEDOM TO CHOOSE

You awake each day with the wonderful right of freedom.

You have the power to choose your daily path and go in the direction of your choosing...you can choose the path of negativity and focus on the things that aren't perfect in your life. You can choose to focus your thoughts on your problems or on the things that you don't have and drag yourself through the mud the entire day.

Or...you can lift your spirits to the sky and focus on all the glorious opportunities you are presented with each and every day...

You can choose to have a positive attitude and focus on a positive action that will strengthen your... values and help you soar like an eagle to new heights.

You have the choice...you have the power...will you soar like an eagle today –

J. CHAREST

The freedom to choose to walk in who you are destined to become is a process, which requires daily change. Each day you must remind yourself of who you are now, instead of allowing your circumstances to dictate who you are.

You are not your yesterday. You must look at your past as just that. You have gone beyond that situation that circumstance. Today gives you a fresh start from your yesterday.

The most important kind of freedom is to be who you really are. You trade in your reality for a role. You trade in your sense for an act, you give up your ability to feel, and in exchange put on a mask. There can't be any large scale revolutions until there is a personal revolution on an individual level. It's got to happen inside first – **JIM MORRISON**

Every person that did anything great was innovated. By faith they moved out on what they could not see and believed that it could happen. Your dreams and visions are housed on the inside of you and while others can say push. Ultimately you are the one that has to bear into the pain. Allow your private areas to be seen and push out the new, fresh, innovated you.

You have to release the dependence on man's approval and depend totally on God's approval. John the Baptist would have never been the fore-runner for Christ if he had been concerned about being accepted.

Matthew 3:4-6MSG

4 John dressed in a camel-hair habit tied at the waist by a leather strap. He lived on a diet of locusts and wild field honey. 5 people poured out of Jerusalem, Judea, and the Jordanian countryside to hear and see him in action. 6 There at the Jordan River those who came to confess their sins were baptized into a changed life.

John didn't dress like everyone else. He didn't eat like everyone else, and his ministry in the desert was a change from the familiar. His mission was to separate people from their religious systems. He was different but they came to see and hear. Regardless of what you are trying to package, it's always the goods on the inside that get the job done. They came to see; but it was the package on the inside that changed them. Dare to be different and make a difference. God wants to cultivate the package on the inside, for His kingdom. Being in a familiar package is like being an empty suit. Let God package you on the inside.

Greatness always has an edge that the norm does not. There is sharpness and precision that places it on the cutting edge above the rest. There is an exchange that has to take place. There is a cutting edge anointing on you. Don't exchange it for the familiar which signifies an edge with no precision, no curve because it's the norm.

Your greatest achievements will not come because you are operating in the norm. But dare to step out of your safety net and see what greatness lies beyond your being accepted by man. Don't be afraid to be you.

For many years of my life I was afraid to be me, always willing to change and adapt for the sake of fitting in. There is a saying if you don't frame your life someone else will. Framing your own life according to God's pattern for you can sometimes be intimidating. It's especially difficult when you have been used to being framed by someone or something else other than who God created you to be.

In times of feeling vulnerable to the old behavior patterns, you must reinforce your mind to whom you have become. Find scripture to support daily affirmations about yourself. This will give you the strength to sustain your new place of freedom.

DISCOVERING YOU

Your freedom is a choice. What are you choosing?

What is the valuable package on the inside?

Find scripture to affirm your new you

Inspired Thoughts...

_____

_____

_____

_____

_____

_____

_____

_____

_____

_____

_____

_____

_____

_____

_____

_____

_____

_____

_____

_____

_____

YOU ARE OF GREAT WORTH

You are priceless. You are of great worth. God has placed uniqueness in you that cannot be compared with anyone else.

Abram had to come out of Abraham – Abraham was there all along waiting on

Abram to be pushed out so that Abraham could come forth, the father of many nations. (Bishop Jakes)

 God is taking out everything that shouldn't be there and he is pouring in everything that you are destined to become.

Saul had to come out so Paul could appear. The fight is always for what is in you. The enemy is not fighting you for where you are but where you are going. God can produce you in a struggle (Bishop Jakes). God will make you what you don't believe is inside of you

My prayer is that after you have read this book, and applied its principles, that you have now entered into a sense of a new life, a true freedom. You have been released from the captivity of a false self, and now walking into a new liberty. You are of great worth. You have been called for such a time as this.

ABOUT THE AUTHOR

Prophetess Jacqueline Rhymes

Prophetess Rhymes has been called to bring radical change to the lives of those that desire to be free from the bondages of sin and defeat through the Word of God. She confronts sloppy Christian living by exposing and unveiling the tactics and schemes of the enemy. God has truly anointed and appointed Prophetess Rhymes as an imminent voice to minister the Gospel with grace and love, dividing asunder the spirits of mediocrity and complacency in order for people to experience the extraordinary manifestation of God's glory. Operating under a keen prophetic mantle, she brings encouragement and healing to the wounded and broken hearted.

In 2011, Prophetess Rhymes birthed *"Boots On the Ground"* Intercessory Prayer Team. *"Boots On the Ground"* is called to respond and engage through fervent intercession, emergency prayer requests day or night.

Through the onset of this ministry, Prophetess Rhymes has seen lives drastically changed by the power of prayer and intercession.

Prophetess Rhymes has also been an influential collaborator of the *"Deborah Company of Chicago"* network. This networking team has a strong passion to see hurting woman come into wholeness and walk in their God given destiny.

Not only is Prophetess a gifted orator, strategist, and entrepreneur, but she is the author of the prophetic manual, entitled *"Understanding the Prophetic©"*. This manual provides in depth revelation knowledge concerning the prophetic office, gift and calling as explored through scripture and is designed to instruct and train leaders in prophetic ministry. Prophetess is often sought out by pastors and leaders to conduct workshops and seminars based on her God-given wisdom and earnest desire to see God's people have a true understanding for this five-fold ministry gift.

Prophetess Jacqueline Rhymes is married to Apostle Kenneth Rhymes Sr. and is the Co-Laborer of Ordained of God Full Gospel Church, in Chicago, IL where she serves in ministry with her husband.

She is the proud mother of three children Aaron, Michelle, and Kenneth Jr. Prophetess Rhymes has been a spiritual mother and mentor to countless people and is affectionately called Mom by many.

CONTACT INFORMATION

ORDAINED OF GOD FULL GOSPEL CHURCH INC.
13750 S. LEYDEN AVE
CHICAGO, IL 60827

E-MAIL ADDRESS ORDAINED2@AOL.COM

www.ingramcontent.com/pod-product-compliance
Lightning Source LLC
Chambersburg PA
CBHW061458040426
42450CB00008B/1407